Illustrator Notes

I am Melanie Guice, and I hope you enjoy my book. I wanted to show how God created the first man and woman. I was excited and wanted to write about the story when I read it. It is amazing how God created the first man out of the dust. Then He made a woman out of the man's rib.
(Children of Color Story Book Bible 2019)

This Book Belongs To

_____

This Book Is Dedicated To:

Thank You, To My Lord and Savior

My Mommy and Daddy
My Sisters and Cousins
My Grandmas and Grandpas
My God Parents
My God Sister
My Church family
My Friends
My Teachers

Special Dedication To:

Dr. Claybon Lea, Jr. my Pastor

GOD MADE ADAM AND EVE

BY: MELANIE GUICE

God's World before He made man.

God took the dust and formed a man.

God made a man his name was Adam

God told Adam You may eat fruit from any tree except the tree of good and evil.

Life

Adam needed help in the world so God decided to make a woman.

God put Adam in a deep sleep.

God made a woman from Adam's rib.

Adam and Eve together in the garden.

The Snake said, "It's ok to eat from the forbidden tree."

Eve took a big bite and handed the fruit to her husband.

Adam took a big bite out of the apple.

Eve said to God the snake told me to do it. So, I ate it and gave one to my husband.

God put a curse on the snake. He would crawl and eat dirt.

God Cursed Eve to suffer during childbirth.

So Adam was forced out of the garden of Eden. He had to work hard the rest of his life, and once he died, he would return to the dust.

Resource Page

Children's of Color Story Book Bible (2019)
Adam and Eve *By Children of Color*

www.ingramcontent.com/pod-product-compliance
Lightning Source LLC
Chambersburg PA
CBHW042005150426
43194CB00002B/131